ANNABEL KARMEL

Mom and Me
COOKBOOK

Have fun in the kitchen!

LONDON, NEW YORK, MUNICH,
MELBOURNE, and DELHI

DK

LONDON, NEW YORK, MUNICH,
MELBOURNE, and DELHI

SENIOR ART EDITOR • Claire Patané
SENIOR EDITOR • Elinor Greenwood
DESIGNER • Sadie Thomas
PHOTOGRAPHER • Dave King
FOOD STYLISTS • Dagmar Vesely,
Caroline Mason

PUBLISHING MANAGER • Sue Leonard
MANAGING ART EDITOR • Clare Shedden
JACKET DESIGNER • Victoria Harvey
PRODUCTION • Alison Lenane
DTP DESIGNER • Almudena Díaz

First American Edition, 2005

Published in the United States by
DK Publishing, Inc., 375 Hudson Street,
New York, New York 10014

05 06 07 08 09   10 9 8 7 6 5 4 3 2 1

A Cataloging-in-Publication record for this book
is available from the Library of Congress.

ISBN: 0-7566-1006-0

Color reproduction by Colourscan
Printed and bound in China by SNP Leefung

Discover more at
www.dk.com

Contents

This is my first book for children. I have chosen recipes that are fun, look and taste fabulous, yet are easy enough for cooks as young as three years old to make.

Children love to cook and relish kneading and rolling out dough or cracking eggs. Cooking with your child is a terrific way of bonding. Also, they learn skills like counting, measuring, weighing, and telling time—all without noticing it.

In this book there are lots of healthy recipes for dips, main meals, and smoothies, as well as yummy desserts. Children will eagerly eat something they have prepared themselves, and take great pride in watching someone else enjoy their food. Also, getting children involved in the kitchen is a great way to motivate picky eaters.

Take time to cook with your child and, above all, have fun in the kitchen!

Annabel Karmel

Things you will need:

Mixing bowl   Knife and fork   Small saucepan   Wooden spoon   Large bowl   Wooden spatula

Sieve   Glasses   Plastic wrap   Rolling pin   Baking sheet   Masher

Muffin pan   Muffin papers   Cookie cutter   Cooling rack   Piping bag   Palette knife

Things you will do:

beat   mix   cream   grate   mash

melt   puree   sift   simmer   whisk

How to knead:

1. Flatten your dough slightly, then fold it over toward you.

2. Press the heels of your hands into the dough and push the dough slightly away from you.

3. Turn the dough through ¼ turn, then fold, press, and turn again. Repeat for about 8 minutes.

Frying pan   Grater   Saucepan with lid   Whisk

Wok   Brush   Square cake pan   Blender

Round cake pan   Straws and skewers   Freezer pop molds   Tall glasses

What things mean:

1. Basic equipment you'll need to make a recipe

2. Number of people served or things made

3. An adult needs to help with this step

It's time to get cracking
and cook some eggs.

sunny scrambled eggs

Simply scramble eggs for
a bright start to the day.

You will need:

salt and
pepper

1 tbsp
butter

2 eggs

2 tbsp
milk

How to make it...

1 Crack the eggs by tapping the shells on the rim of a bowl. Then split the eggs open.

2 Whisk the eggs together with a pinch of salt and pepper.

3 Melt the butter over medium heat. Pour in the eggs and milk and keep stirring.

4 Two minutes later, when the mixture has thickened and looks set, spoon it onto a plate.

Serve buttery "rays" of toast around your egg.

my favorite crêpes

A foolproof crêpe batter—no flops when you flip these!

You will need:

1 cup flour

a big pinch of salt

2 eggs

1 cup milk

¼ cup water

4 tbsp butter

strawberries

blueberries

raspberries

maple syrup

How to make them...

1 Sift the flour and salt into a mixing bowl. Then make a well in the center of the flour.

2 Break the eggs into the well. Whisk the eggs and flour together. Next, mix together the water and milk in a separate bowl or large measuring cup.

3 Add the liquid to the flour, a little at a time, whisking to make a smooth batter. Melt 2 tbsp of the butter and stir it into the batter. Strain if lumpy.

4 Melt butter in a small frying pan. Get the pan really hot, then turn down the heat to medium.

5 Add the batter— you'll need about 2 tbsp for each crêpe. Tilt the pan so the batter covers the base.

6 Cook the crêpe for about one minute. Use a spatula to loosen it, then flip it over! Cook the second side for 30 seconds.

7 Fill the crêpes with fresh fruit and plenty of maple syrup.

slurpy spaghetti

Serve with tomato sauce and get your taste buds zinging.

You will need:

2 tbsp olive oil

½ tbsp tomato paste

½ tsp balsamic vinegar

½ tsp sugar

14-oz (400-g) can of chopped tomatoes

1 onion, peeled and chopped

7 oz (200 g) spaghetti

1 clove garlic, crushed

salt and pepper

Parmesan cheese

How to make it...

1 Heat the oil in a pan. Add the onion and garlic and fry over medium heat for 5 minutes or until the onion is see-through and soft.

2 Add the canned tomatoes, tomato paste, balsamic vinegar, sugar, and a pinch of salt and pepper. Cover with a lid and simmer for about 20 minutes.

3 **Cook the spaghetti** in a large pan of boiling water. Check the package to see how long to cook it.

4 **Grate the Parmesan cheese,** keeping your fingers safely away from the grater! Drain the pasta, put it into bowls, and top with the tomato sauce.

Sprinkle with the grated cheese and get slurping!

perfect pasta

Pass the pasta! This dish is quick and easy to prepare.

4 tbsp honey

2 tbsp rice wine vinegar

2 tbsp soy sauce

1 tbsp sesame oil

You will need:

2 cooked chicken breasts

1 cup sweet corn

2 green onions

2 cups broccoli

7 oz (200 g) pasta shapes

How to make it...

1 Cook the pasta shapes according to the package directions. Add the broccoli for the last 3 minutes.

2 Tear the cooked chicken into bite-sized pieces. Remove any pieces of skin.

3 **Carefully slice** the green onions.

4 **Make a dressing** by mixing together the honey, rice wine vinegar, soy sauce, and sesame oil.

5 **Mix together** the pasta, broccoli, chicken, green onions, sweet corn, and dressing.

6 **Dish it up.** Your pasta salad is now ready to eat.

in

Learn to make
pizza dough,
then two tiptop
toppings...

pizza
dough

You will need:

1½ tsp dried yeast

1 tsp sugar

2 tbsp olive oil, plus extra for oiling

1 cup warm water

2¾ cups bread flour, plus extra for sprinkling

salt and pepper

How to make it...

1 **Mix the yeast** with 3 tbsp water. Set this aside for 10 minutes or until it is frothy.

2 **Sift the flour** into a bowl and add the sugar, salt, and pepper. Then make a well in the center.

3 **Pour the yeast,** water, and oil into the well. Use your hands to mix everything together.

4 **Sprinkle flour** over a clean work surface. Then knead the dough for 8 minutes, until it is smooth and elastic.

5 **Oil a large bowl,** put in the dough, and cover with plastic wrap. Leave in a warm place until the dough has doubled in size.

6 **Is it ready?** Poke holes in the dough. If the holes stay, it's ready. Punch down with your fists and place on a floured surface.

2-in-1 pizzas

Get arty with your pizzas and make them look like faces.
Or add chicken for a finger-licking feast.

You will need:

your pizza dough

pizza sauce

1 cooked chicken breast, diced

pepperoni

green onions

diced ham

sweet peppers

mushrooms

basil

sliced pitted olives

grated cheese

cherry tomatoes

How to make them...

1 **Knead the dough again.**
Then cut it into four equal pieces.
Roll each piece into a 7-in (18-cm) circle
and place on a baking sheet.

2 **Preheat the oven**
to 425°F (220°C). Spread pizza
sauce on each pizza base.

3 **Make faces** on your pizzas using your favorite toppings. Try tomato noses, olive eyes, sweet pepper hair, or any other combination.

4 **Spoon chicken,** sliced green onions, and sweet peppers onto your pizzas for an alternative treat.

5 **Sprinkle cheese** all over your pizzas. Then cook them in the oven for 12 minutes or until golden and bubbling.

potato mice

These baked-potato mice are almost too gorgeous to eat!

You will need:
radishes
cherry tomatoes
raisins
green onions
chives
4 potatoes
salt and pepper
1 tbsp oil
1/3 cup milk
2 tbsp butter
grated cheese

How to make them...

1 Wash the potatoes and pat them dry. Prick the skins with a fork and put the potatoes on a baking sheet. Brush them all over with oil.

2 Bake the potatoes until they are soft. Medium-sized potatoes take about one hour in an oven preheated to 400°F (200°C).

3 Cool enough to handle? Then cut off the tops and carefully scoop out the soft potato centers. You can throw away the tops (or eat them).

4 Mash the soft centers with the butter, milk, and cheese. Add a pinch of salt and pepper, then put the mixture back into the potato skins.

5 Sprinkle with cheese
and cook your potatoes under the
broiler for a few minutes until golden.

6 Make a nose and whiskers
with half a tomato held in place with
a toothpick and chives tucked behind it.

7 Finish decorating
with raisin eyes, radish
ears, and green onion tails.

sweet-and-sour chicken

This recipe is a great favorite, and it always looks pretty and colorful.

You will need:

8 oz (250 g) diced chicken breast

⅔ cup carrot matchsticks

2 tbsp sliced green onions

1 cup sliced baby corn

1 cup white rice

1 cup trimmed green beans

4 tbsp vegetable oil

Batter:

1 egg yolk

black pepper

1½ tbsp corn starch

1 tbsp milk

Sauce:

1 tbsp soy sauce

4 tbsp chicken stock

2 tbsp rice wine vinegar

2 tbsp ketchup

2 tbsp superfine sugar

How to make it...

1 **Start cooking** the rice according to the directions on the package.

2 **Make the sauce** by mixing together all the sauce ingredients in a bowl.

3 **Beat together** the batter ingredients in another bowl.

4 **Dip the chicken** in batter, then fry it in 2 tbsp of oil over medium heat. Remove from the pan.

5 **Next, stir-fry** the carrots, baby corn, and beans in the remaining 2 tbsp of oil for 4 minutes.

6 **Add the sauce** and boil for 1 minute. Then add the chicken and green onions and heat through.

7 **Dish it up.** Spoon a helping of sweet-and-sour chicken on top of a bed of rice.

avocado frog dip

Cause a stir with this froggy dip. Choose your favourite vegetables to go with it... Gribbit!

You will need:

1 large avocado

1 tomato

1 tbsp of lemon juice

2 tbsp of sour cream

chives

salt and pepper

cucumber slices

stuffed olives

carrot batons

cucumber sticks

strips of pitta bread

red pepper slices

1 **Cut the avocado** in half, remove the stone from the middle and scoop out the flesh.

2 **Squeeze lemon** juice onto the avocado to help it keep its colour. One tablespoon is enough.

3 **Mash up** the avocado and lemon juice and mix it with the sour cream.

4 **Chop the tomato** into tiny pieces. Snip 1 ½ tbsp chives. Mix these with the mash.

5 **Season the dip** with a grinding of salt and pepper.

Gribbit!

6 **Make a frog face** on your dip using sliced cucumber and olives for eyes and chives for a mouth.

fishy fruit dip

Serve this dip with skewers of your favorite fruit.

You will need:

1 mango
(or 1 peach)

²/₃ cup plain yogurt

chocolate chips

mandarin segments

1 tsp honey

kiwi and apple slices

How to make it...

1 **First cut up the mango** by slicing it in half and cutting the flesh into cubes. Gently turn the skin inside out and cut off the cubes.

2 **Mash the mango** in a bowl. Use a fork or potato masher to make the mango into a smooth pulp.

3 Mix the mango
with the yogurt and add honey to sweeten.

4 Decorate the dip
with a mandarin mouth, chocolate chip eye, and kiwi fruit and apple fins and tail.

5 Make fruity dip sticks
by threading chunks of your favorite fruits onto skewers. Then get dipping!

melon

grape

strawberry

pineapple

quick and easy cupcakes

Soft, moist cupcakes—they're as easy as...

1

2

3.

You will need:

2 large eggs

1 tsp vanilla extract

²⁄₃ cup superfine sugar

½ cup soft butter

1 cup self-rising flour

How to make them...

1 **Preheat the oven** to 350°F (180°C). Put all the ingredients in a bowl and beat together until the mixture is smooth and slightly lighter in color.

2 **Line a muffin pan** with muffin papers and half-fill each paper with the cupcake batter.

3 **Bake the cakes** for 18 to 20 minutes. You can tell they are done when they have risen up, are golden in color, and spring back into shape when pressed.

cupcake farm

Decorate your cupcakes and make the sweetest little animals.

You will need:

your cupcakes

2½ cups powdered sugar

cookies

chocolate buttons

colorful candies

1 stick (8 tbsp) butter, softened

1 tbsp water

red food coloring

marshmallows (including mini marshmallows)

tubes of writing icing

1 Make the butter frosting.

Sift the powdered sugar into a bowl. In another bowl, beat the butter until creamy. Gradually add the powdered sugar to the butter, beating to keep the mixture smooth. Finally, beat in the water.

2 Make marshmallow sheep. Spread a thick layer of butter frosting over the top of the cupcakes.

3 Stick on marshmallows, using large ones for faces, halved ones for ears, and mini ones for woolly coats.

4 Make pink piggies by mixing a few drops of red food coloring with the butter frosting. Spread the pink frosting on top of the cupcakes.

5 Stick on a nose made from a large marshmallow and ears made from slices of marshmallow.

6 To make puppy cakes, spread on the frosting, then stick on cookie ears and candy eyes and noses.

7 Draw the faces on your animals using writing icing squeezed from a tube.

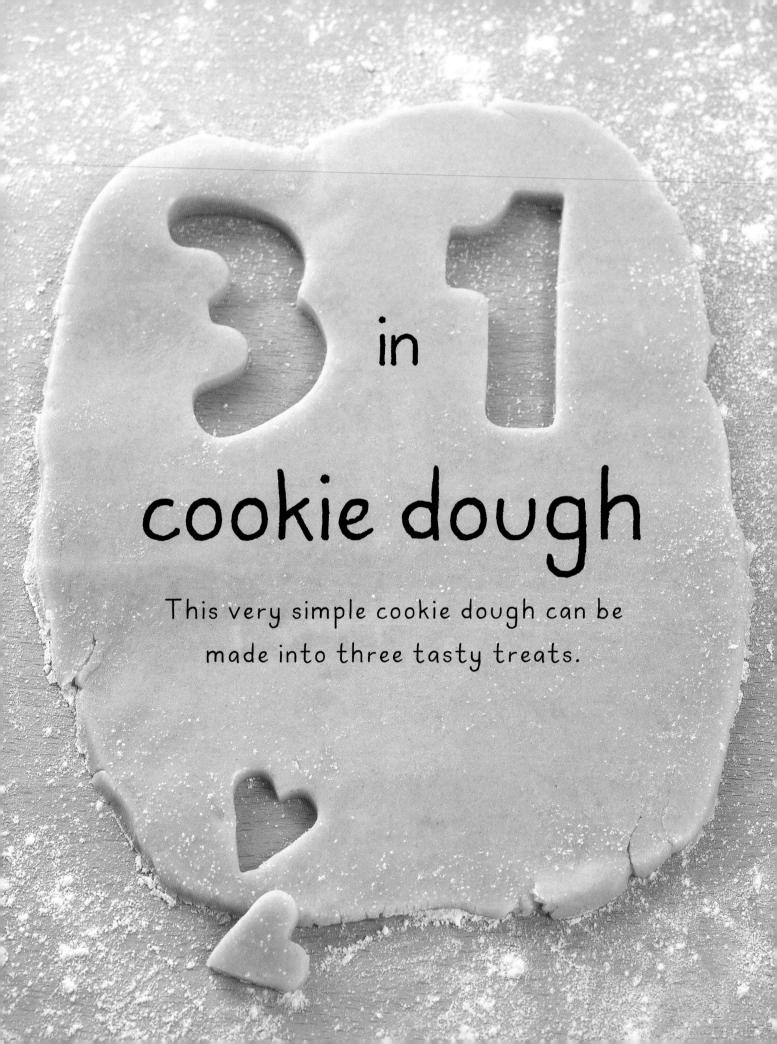

3 in 1

in

cookie dough

This very simple cookie dough can be
made into three tasty treats.

You will need:

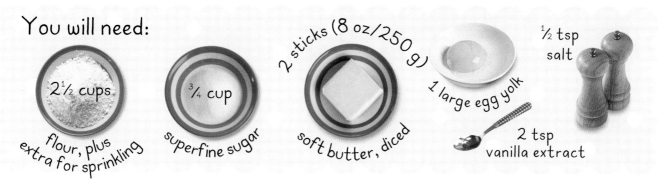

2½ cups flour, plus extra for sprinkling

¾ cup superfine sugar

2 sticks (8 oz/250 g) soft butter, diced

1 large egg yolk

2 tsp vanilla extract

½ tsp salt

How to make it...

1 Beat the butter and sugar together in a bowl.

2 Add the egg yolk and vanilla extract and beat the mixture until it is smooth.

3 Next, add the flour and salt and mix everything together to form a smooth dough.

4 Mold the dough into a ball, wrap it in plastic wrap, and refrigerate for 30 minutes.

animal cookies

Here's how to turn your dough
into a crowd of cookie creatures.

You will need:

1 cup powdered sugar, sifted

1 tbsp water

your cookie dough

writing icing

1 tbsp cocoa powder

How to make them...

1 **Preheat the oven**
to 350°F (180°C).
Divide the dough in half.
Make one half chocolate by
kneading in the cocoa powder.

2 **Roll the dough**
out to about ¼ in
(5 mm) thick on a surface
sprinkled with flour.

3 **Cut out animals.**
Put them on nonstick
or lined baking sheets. Roll
out leftover dough and cut
out more animals.

4 **Bake the cookies** for 12 minutes or until golden. Leave them on a wire rack to cool.

5 **Make icing** by mixing together the powdered sugar and water. Pipe the icing onto the cookies to decorate.

6 **Draw on faces** and other features using writing icing squeezed from a tube.

Animal cookies are great served with cold milk.

....baa

jam sweethearts

Show someone how much you love them with these yummy jam cookies.

You will need:

your cookie dough

4 tbsp softened butter, plus extra for greasing

1 cup powdered sugar, sifted

jelly or jam

a few drops of vanilla extract

1 tsp water

How to make them...

1 **Preheat the oven** to 350°F (180°C). Roll out dough to ¼ in (5 mm) thick. Cut out circles with a 2½-in (6-cm) cutter.

2 **Arrange circles** on greased baking sheets. Cut hearts from half your cookie circles using a 1-in (2.5-cm) cutter.

3 **Bake the cookies** for 12 minutes or until golden. Let them cool completely.

4 Make the butter frosting by beating the butter until smooth, then gradually beating in the powdered sugar, water, and vanilla extract. Spread frosting over the whole (not heart) cookies.

5 Now spoon on the jam. Drop a small spoonful of jam on top of the butter frosting. Put the heart cookies on top. Now eat them—yum!

rolled cookies

Rolling right along! Make chocolate and cranberry spirals.

You will need:

a few drops of red food coloring

your cookie dough

2 tbsp chopped dried cranberries

1 tbsp cocoa powder

How to make them...

1 **Divide the dough** in four. Color one piece brown by kneading in cocoa powder. Color another pink with cranberries and food coloring. Leave two plain.

2 **Wrap the dough** in plastic wrap. Put it in the refrigerator for about 30 minutes. Preheat the oven to 350°F (180°C).

3 **Roll the dough** out on a floured surface. Each piece of dough should make a rectangle about 7 x 8 in (18 x 20 cm).

4 **For rolled cookies** place the plain dough on the chocolate dough. Trim the edges and roll into a log. Repeat with the pink dough.

5 **Marbled cookies** are made from all the dough trimmings. Simply knead them together, then roll them into a log.

6 **Slice the logs** into ¼-in (5-mm) slices. Put the slices on nonstick or lined baking sheets.

7 **Now bake** your cookies for 15 to 18 minutes or until lightly golden.

chocolate fridge cake

These delicious bricks of chocolate cake will keep for two weeks in the refrigerator.

You will need:

8 oz (250 g) graham crackers

5 oz (150 g) semisweet chocolate

5 oz (150 g) milk chocolate

½ cup golden syrup or light corn syrup

1 stick (8 tbsp) unsalted butter

½ cup raisins

¾ cup dried apricots, chopped

½ cup chopped pecans (optional)

How to make it...

1 Use plastic wrap to line an 8-in (20-cm) square pan. Leave extra plastic wrap hanging over the sides.

2 Break the crackers into pieces with a rolling pin. (Put them in a plastic bag first so they don't go everywhere!)

3 Melt chocolate, butter, and syrup in a heatproof bowl set over a pan of simmering water. Stir occasionally.

4 **Remove the bowl** from the heat and stir in the broken crackers, apricots, raisins, and pecans (optional).

5 **Spoon the mix** into the pan. Level the surface by pressing it down with a potato masher.

6 **Allow to cool,** then put the chocolate mixture in the refrigerator for 1 to 2 hours to set.

7 **Turn out the cake** and peel off the plastic wrap. Cut the cake into 12 squares and enjoy!.

raspberry ripple cheesecake

Swirl raspberries and cream to make the dreamiest cheesecake ever!

You will need:

1 stick (8 tbsp) butter

8 oz (250 g) graham crackers

1 tsp vanilla extract

16 oz (450 g) cream cheese

1 cup superfine sugar

2½ cups fresh raspberries

⅔ cup powdered sugar

1⅔ cups whipping cream

How to make it...

1 Put the crackers in a bag. Then use a rolling pin to roll and crush them into crumbs.

2 Melt the butter in a pan. Pour the crushed graham crackers into the butter and stir thoroughly.

3 Line an 8-in (20-cm) cake pan (one with a removable base) with plastic wrap. Spoon in the cracker mixture, press flat with a masher, and refrigerate.

4 Make raspberry puree— bring the raspberries and powdered sugar to a boil, then simmer for 10 minutes. Cool, then press through a sieve.

5 Mix together the cream cheese, superfine sugar, and vanilla extract. Whip the cream until stiff, then fold it into the cheese mixture.

6 Spread topping on the cracker base— use about ¾ of the cheese mixture. Then spoon on ¾ of the puree and swirl it into the cheesecake mixture.

7 Gently spread on the remaining cheesecake mixture. Drizzle on straight lines of raspberry puree. Pull a skewer across the lines for a feathered effect.

Leave the cheesecake in the refrigerator for at least 2 hours or overnight.

peach melba shakeup

You'll be all shook up with
this perfect pick-me-up!

How to make it...

You will need:

2½ cups
peach slices

1 cup
raspberries

1 cup
raspberry yogurt

1 Get rid of the seeds
by pressing the raspberries
through a sieve.

2 Blend the raspberries,
peach (except two slices), and yogurt.
Serve decorated with the reserved peach.

coconut dream

This is a creamy drink
with a tropical taste.

You will need:

½ cup
coconut milk

1¼ cups
pineapple juice

2 scoops
ice cream

⅔ cup pineapple
chunks

1 First blend, then pour.
Put the coconut milk, pineapple juice, ice
cream, and pineapple (except two chunks) into a
blender and blend. Pour the drink into glasses
and serve with the reserved pineapple.

summertime smoothie

This is fruity and refreshing on hot days.

You will need:

2 peaches   1 banana   ½ cup strawberries   vanilla yog...   orange j...

How to make it...

1 First, prepare the fruit. Peel and slice the banana and peaches. Remove the green leaves from most of the strawberries. Cut the strawberries into slices.

2 Push strawberry slices and banana slices onto straws. Put the other fruit in a blender and blend. Pour the drink into glasses and serve with the straws of fruit.

summertime smoothie

coconut dream

peach melba shakeup

traffic light freezer pops

Red, yellow, green—
let's go and eat!

You will need:

3 large ripe peaches

½ cup superfine sugar

5 large ripe kiwi fruits

¼ small watermelon

3 tbsp water

How to make them...

1 For the red, remove the melon seeds. Puree the flesh in a blender with ⅓ of the sugar. Pour the puree into freezer pop molds so they are all ⅓ full. Freeze for 1½ hours.

2 For the yellow, peel the peaches. Blend the flesh with another ⅓ of the sugar. Pour this yellow puree onto the frozen red puree so the molds are now ⅔ full. Freeze until solid.

3 For the green, peel the kiwi fruits. Blend with the water and the remaining sugar. Press the puree through a sieve to get rid of the seeds. Fill the molds, then add the sticks and freeze.

berry nice pops

Enjoy hot days licking cool freezer pops!

You will need:

1 cup raspberries

juice of 2 medium oranges

¼ cup water

¼ cup superfine sugar

1½ cups strawberries, hulled and cut in half

zoom!

How to make them...

1 **Boil the sugar** and water in a pan. Stir constantly until the sugar is dissolved.

2 **Puree and strain** the strawberries and raspberries. Mix with the sugar water and orange juice.

3 **Pour the mixture** into freezer pop molds. Put in the sticks and freeze until solid.

chocolate sundae

Here's a sweet dessert that couldn't be easier to make.

You will need:

2 chocolate muffins

3 tbsp half-and-half

2 scoops vanilla ice cream

2-oz (60-g) chocolate-caramel candy bar

1 Melt the candy bar in a bowl set over a pan of hot water. Add the cream and stir to make a smooth sauce.

2 Scoop out the tops of the muffins. Spoon on the vanilla ice cream, then pour on the caramel sauce and enjoy!

strawberry cream surprise

This no-cook treat is crunchy and smooth—and deliciously sweet.

You will need:
4 small scoops of strawberry ice cream

sprigs of mint

2 meringue shells

½ pint of strawberries

1 Break meringue into small pieces. Hull the strawberries. Mash half of them and slice the rest.

2 Fill two glasses with layers of mashed and sliced strawberries, ice cream, and meringue pieces.

3 Finish off with a spoonful of ice cream and mashed strawberries. Decorate each glass with a sprig of mint, then serve.

Index

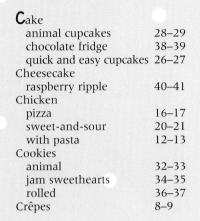

Annabel Karmel is a leading author on cooking for children and has written 12 best-selling books that are sold all over the world.

She is an expert in devising tasty and nutritious meals for children without the need for parents to spend hours in the kitchen.

Annabel writes regularly for British newspapers including *The Times* and the *Daily Mail* and appears frequently on radio and television as the UK's expert on children's nutritional issues.

annabel karmel

Visit Annabel's website
www.annabelkarmel.com

Thank you

Acknowledgments

With thanks to the children who took part in the photography:

Arabella Earley (MOT Junior Agency), Emily Wigoder, Euan Thomson, and Harry Holmstoel (Norrie Carr Agency)

Thanks also to Penny Arlon, Penny Smith, and Wendy Bartlet for editorial and design work on this book